HOBBYCRAFT
FOR JUNIORS

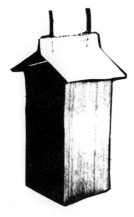

HOBBYCRAFT
FOR JUNIORS
Willard & Elma Waltner

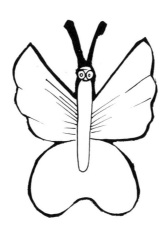

LANTERN PRESS, INC., *Publishers*

257 Park Avenue South

New York, N. Y. 10010

The following used by permission of Summertime, from article "Wind Whimsies", copyright by Scholastic Magazines, Inc. 1966; Wind Tinkler

The following used by permission of UPWARD, copyright by the Baptist Sunday School Board, 1965; Madam Whisk

The following used by permission of Boy's Life, copyright by The Boy Scouts of America, 1966; Tan's Picture Puzzle Cards

The following used by permission of Five/Six, copyright by The Methodist Publishing House, 1966; Fanny Soap Fish

The following used by permission of Workbasket, copyright by Modern Handcraft, 1966; Flowering Spring Branch

Library of Congress Catalog Card Number 67-12009

Published simultaneously in Canada by
George J. McLeod, Ltd. Toronto
Manufactured in the United States of America

To Christopher

The youngest member of our "do it yourself" family.

FOREWORD

Hello all you boys and girls who like to "make things." We know you do or you wouldn't be reading this book.

Here are directions for all sorts of interesting projects you can make "just for fun" or to use as gifts.

These are easy to assemble and many of them need only materials that would otherwise end up in the trash can.

Some are nice to take to a friend who is ill. Why not get your friends together and have a "making session" of small gifts for folks in a rest home or the children's ward in the hospital. Deliver the things "in person." You will agree that the pleasure of making things is doubled when it is shared.

Have as much fun making the things shown in this book as we did planning them and telling you how.

The Authors.

TABLE OF CONTENTS *Page*

HOBBYCRAFT FOR JUNIORS

TRINKET BOX

You Will Need:

A sour cream or cottage cheese carton

Crepe paper

Corrugated cardboard (the side of a grocery carton is fine)

White glue (Elmer's—Gluebird or other)

How to Make It:

Wash and dry the carton. Scrape the heavy wax coating from the outside with a table knife.

Slip the fold of crepe paper out of its wrapper for about 1 inch. Cut off the strip of paper across the fold, using the edge of the wrapper as a guide to cut straight.

Stretch and lightly twist the strip of paper between the thumbs and fingers of both hands. When you finish the strip will look much like raffia.

Spread glue around the bottom of the carton in a band about 1/2 inch wide.

Beginning at the bottom edge, wind the paper raffia around and around the carton until the glue-covered part is covered with rows of paper. Push the rows close together so none of the carton shows between them. Fig. 1.

Spread on another band of glue and continue wrapping. Wrap the carton until the crepe paper raffia is against the round rim at the top of the carton. Cut off the extra raffia and press the end tight against the carton.

Turn the carton upside down on the corrugated cardboard. Draw around the rim. Cut out this circle for the lid.

Cut a second circle, a little smaller than the first, to fit inside the top of the carton.

Cut a strip of crepe paper 1 inch wide and long enough to reach around the lid circle. Glue the center of one end of the strip to the edge of the cardboard circle. Stretch the crepe paper as you pull it around the cardboard circle. Glue the end in place.

Glue the edges of the strip to the top and bottom of the cardboard circle, Fig. 2.

Cover the edge of the smaller circle the same way. Glue the two circles together, Fig. 3.

Cover the top of the lid with crepe paper raffia. Begin at the center and glue the raffia to the lid in a flat spiral until you reach the outer edge, Fig. 4.

Twist a short piece of raffia of another color into a tight cord. Cut pieces of the cord and glue them to the top of the lid, shaping them into letters to "print" your name.

Mix a teaspoonful of white glue and a teaspoonful of water in a cup. Brush the glue-water mixture on the outside of the box and on the lid. When it dries the raffia covering will be stiff and your trinket box ready to use.

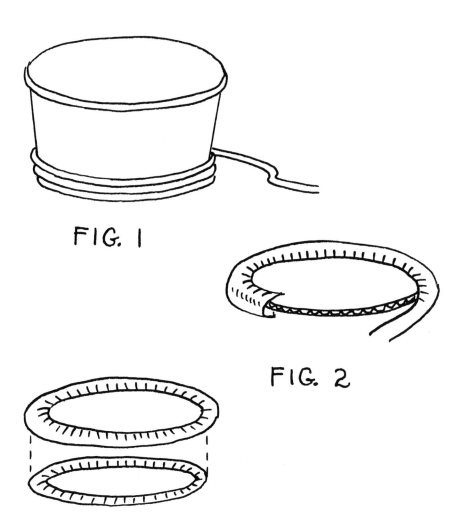

FIG. 1

FIG. 2

FIG. 3

FIG. 4

11

BOUQUET HEADBAND

You will be wearing a bouquet in your hair when you decorate a plain plastic headband with bright felt flowers.

You Will Need:

A plastic headband

Felt scraps

White glue (Elmer's—Gluebird or other)

Household cement (Duco—Testor's or other)

How to Make It:

For the flower petals choose two colors of felt that go well with the color of the headband you are using. Use yellow for the centers, green for the leaves.

Patterns are given for two kinds of flowers. Use these or make some of your own that look like other kinds of posies.

Suppose the headband is brown and you choose pink and blue for the flowers. Cut the larger petals of blue, the smaller size of pink (or the other way around if you wish). Use white glue to fasten the pink petals to the blue ones, with a border of blue all around.

Glue on the yellow centers. Glue the green leaves to the under sides of the flowers with the tips sticking out at the sides.

Make five flowers with leaves.

Fasten a flower to the center of the headband with household cement. Add two more flowers on each side of the center.

Use pinch clothespins to hold the flowers tight against the headband until the cement dries.

FULL SIZE PATTERNS

FLOWERS

LEAVES   CENTERS

PUT THEM TOGETHER
LIKE THIS

AN ORIENTAL FAN

Japanese fans are made of silk or rice paper with painted designs of flowers, birds or scenes. You can make a dainty fan that looks much like an oriental one, only it does not fold flat as most of those do.

You Will Need:

Greeting cards (Birthday cards with flowers are nice)

A popsickle stick for the handle White glue Scotch tape

How to Make It:

Choose greeting cards of lightweight paper folded lengthwise and then crosswise in what is called a "french fold" rather than cards of stiff paper folded only once.

Open a card flat. As you look at it, the part that was the inside of the card is right side up, but the part that was the cover of the card is upside down. Cut the card apart along the crosswise crease. Turn the cover part right side up and glue it to the inside piece, with the edges lapped 1/2 inch. The card is now one piece of paper. It should be about four times as long as it is wide. If you wish, you may use only the covers of several cards, glued together to make a strip four times as long as it is wide.

Beginning at one end, fold 1/2 inch of the card back against itself and crease the fold, Fig. 1.

Fold again, in the other direction, to make a second 1/2 inch wide pleat. Keep folding, first in one direction, then in the other, making 1/2 inch pleats across the strip of paper—Fig. 2—until the whole strip is pleated.

For the handle, glue 1 inch of the popsickle stick into the center pleat.

Gather the pleats on both sides, tight against the popsickle stick. Wrap scotch tape tightly around the gathered pleats to hold them against the popsickle stick handle, Fig. 3.

Spread the pleats into a half circle to finish the fan.

16

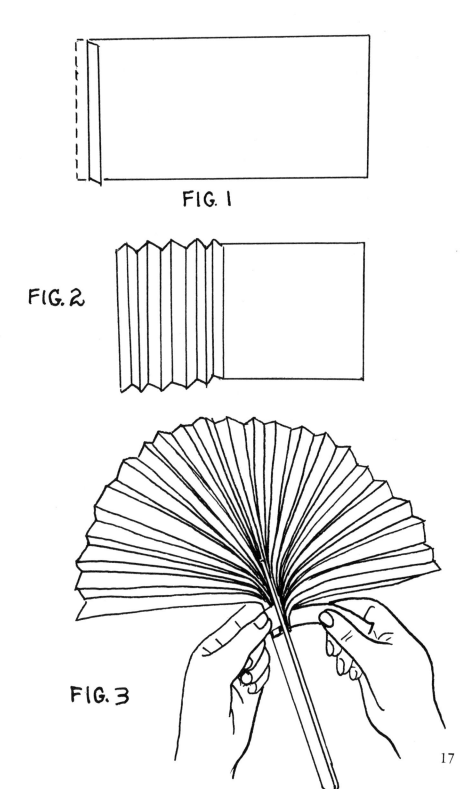

FIG. 1

FIG. 2

FIG. 3

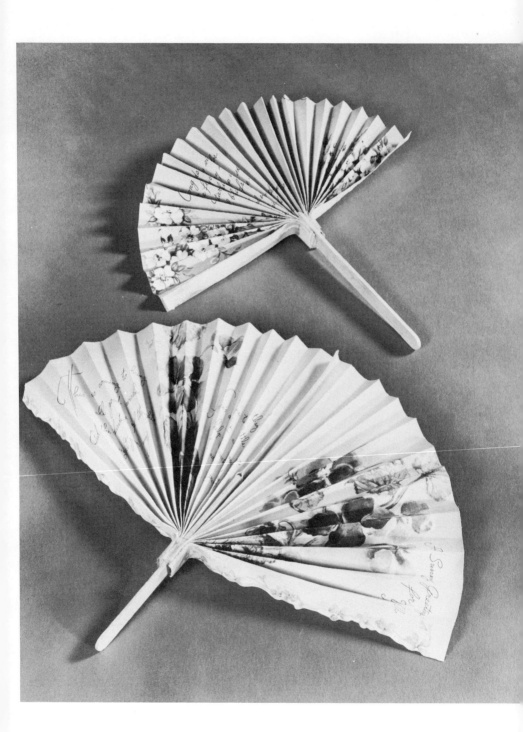

WATER LILY NUTCUP PLACE CARDS

Next time somebody at your house has a birthday, make nutcup place cards and turn your family dinner into a party.

You Will Need:

Colored paper napkins (luncheon size)

Light green construction paper   White glue

How to Make It:

Open the napkin flat. Bring corner 1 to corner 3. Crease along the diagonal fold. Open flat again.

Bring corner 2 to corner 4 and crease the diagonal fold.

Open the napkin flat once more. The center of the napkin is where the crease lines cross each other, as in Fig. 1.

Bring the corners 1, 2, 3, 4, to the center and crease the four slant folds, Fig. 2.

Bring the corners 5, 6, 7, 8 to the center and again crease the slant folds, Fig. 3.

Once more, bring the corners 9, 10, 11, 12, to the center and crease the folds.

Turn the napkin over and fold the corners to the center one more time. It will look like Fig. 4.

Hold the last folds in place with your left hand. With the right hand, reach under and bring up the first layer of points, one at a time, Fig. 5. Bring up the second layer of points, then the third, to make the nutcup that looks like a water lily.

Cut the lily pad from light green construction paper, the shape shown in Fig. 6. It should measure about 2 1/2 inches across.

Glue the nutcup to the lily pad, letting the pad stick out about 1/2 inch at one side.

Print the name on the lily pad, Fig. 7.

Make a nutcup place card for each person and, just for fun, place them around the table "mixed up" from the way your family usually is seated for meals.

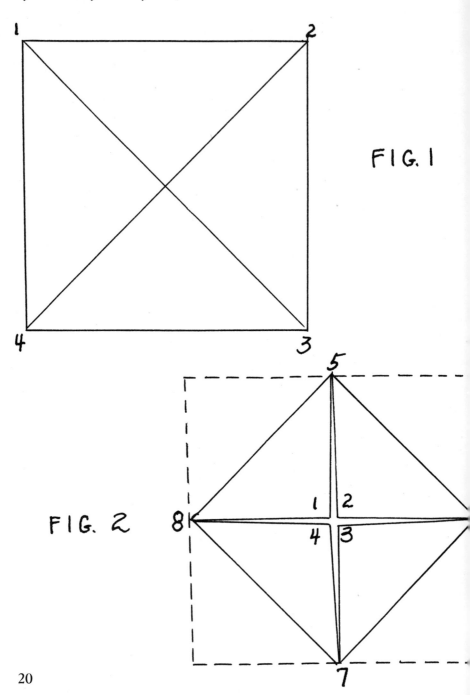

FIG. 1

FIG. 2

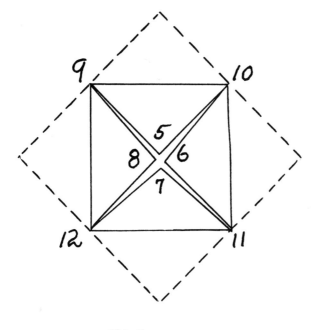

FIG. 3

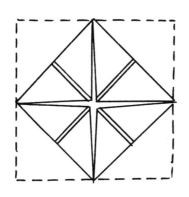

FIG. 4

21

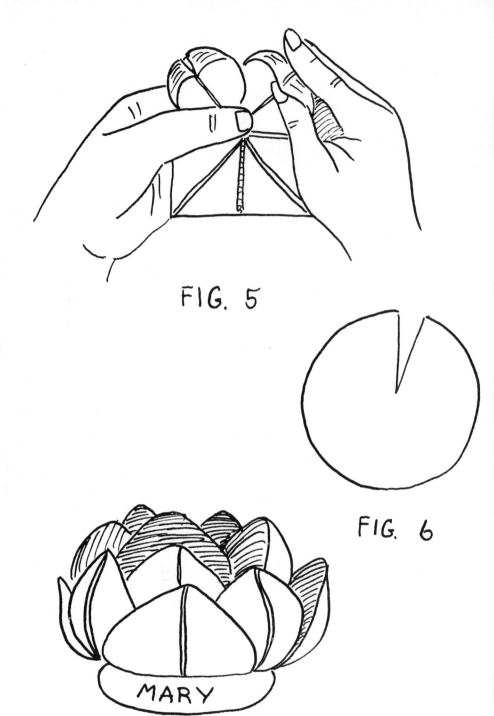

FIG. 5

FIG. 6

MARY

FIG. 7

MANY-COLORED BEADS

Beads made of paper? Who ever heard of such a thing! Until you make some, it's hard to believe how pretty and "different" these are.

You Will Need:

Large magazine covers with brightly colored pictures

Black construction paper

White glue   Clear nail polish   Needle and thread

How to Make Them:

Cut the magazine covers into strips, each 3/4 inch wide.

Cut each strip into a long triangle like that shown in the top drawing of Fig. 1.

Also cut the sheet of black construction paper into strips, some 3/4 inch wide, some 1/2 inch wide. Shape some into triangles as you did the magazine cover, leave the rest as in the lower drawing of Fig. 1.

Place the magazine cover strips, colored side down. Beginning at the wide end, wrap each one tightly around a toothpick, and glue down the tip, as shown in Fig. 2.

Roll the construction paper strips around the toothpick to make black beads. The straight strips make cylinder shaped beads instead of tapered ones like those made from the long triangles.

Coat each bead with clear nail polish. When it is dry, brush on a second coat to make the beads stiff and shiny.

If you want beads of different sizes, make some strips shorter than others. For extra large beads, glue two strips together before cutting triangles.

String the beads on heavy thread, making the string long enough to slip over your head. Tie the ends of the thread together in a square knot. Pass the ends back through two beads, and clip off the extra thread.

When you use beads of different sizes to make a necklace, thread each end of the stringing cord into the eye of a needle. Begin by putting the center bead on first. String the rest of the beads, matching them on each side of the center, one at a time, until the string is as long as you want it, Fig. 3.

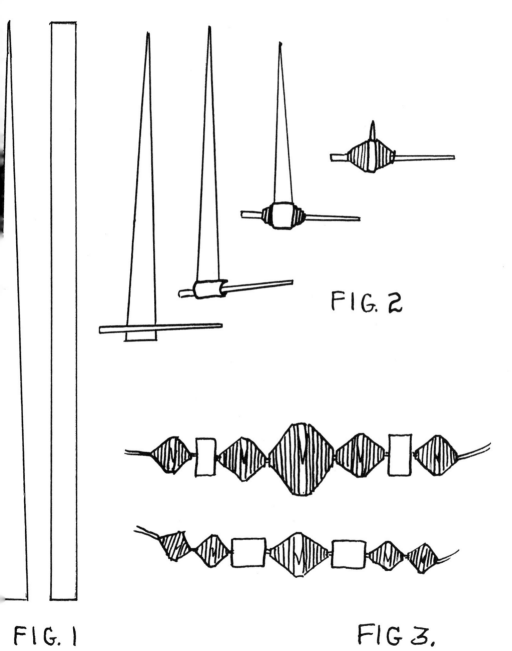

FIG. 2

FIG. 1

FIG 3.

TIN CAN TOM TOM

This is an easy-to-make drum for your sidewalk parades.

You Will Need:

A 5 pound syrup can

Paper for covering

Wrapping cord

A small sponge rubber ball   White glue

A pencil, or 1/4 inch diameter dowel, 10 inches long

How to Make It:

Cut the covering paper 17 inches long, 5 1/2 inches wide. Glue the paper around the can.

Cut a circle of paper to fit the lid. Print the name of your band on it, or decorate it any way you like. Glue the circle to the lid.

If there is no printing on the lid you need not glue on the paper circle. Paint the decorations right on the tin, using colored nail polish or your hobby enamels.

Cut a piece of wrapping cord about 5 feet long, for the neck strap. Wrap the ends of the cord around the can, against the top and bottom rims. Tie tightly in a square knot, Fig. 1. If this makes too long a neck strap, use a shorter piece of cord.

Make the drumstick from the rubber ball and pencil (or dowel). Punch a hole into the ball with a nail or an awl. Sharpen the pencil to a point and work it into the hole, Fig. 2. The sponge rubber will grip it tight and keep the handle from slipping out.

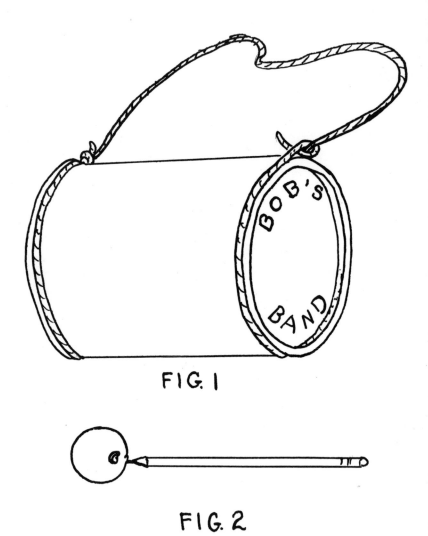

FIG. 1

FIG. 2

CATCH 'EM

How good are you at catching things? Make this little gadget and see.

You Will Need:

    A small tin can—a baby food can is fine

    String—30 inches long

    A large spool

    Paper to cover the can

    White glue

How to Make It:

    Wash and dry the can. Cover the outside with fancy paper, or paint it with your hobby enamels.

    Run a line of glue around the can just below the top rim.

    Wrap one end of the string twice around the can, on the line of glue, and knot it around the free string.

    Slip the other end of the string through the hole in the spool and tie it around the spool. Put a little glue on both knots so they will not come untied. Fig. 1 shows the can with the spool tied to it.

    Hold the can in front of you and let the spool hang down. Swing the spool forward and up. Try to catch it in the can as it falls.

    It's not as easy as it sounds.

    Time yourself to see how long it takes.

    Take turns with a friend, allowing five tries each time, with each catch scoring five points. Play three turns for a game.

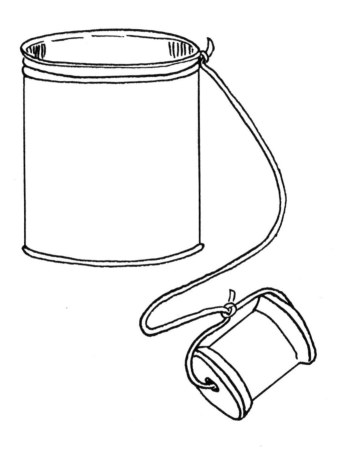

FIG. 1

SCRAP BAG PICTURE

There's a whole flower garden in your mother's sewing scrap bag. Pick yourself a basket of posies and hang them on your wall.

You Will Need:

Bright colored scraps of cloth

Rickrack or other fancy braid

A piece of cardboard 8 1/2 inches by 9 1/2 inches

Black construction paper, same size as the cardboard

Waxed paper drinking straws   White glue

How to Make It:

Glue the construction paper to the cardboard.

Flatten eight drinking straws by squeezing them between your thumb and forefinger. Glue two along the top edge of the black paper, moving them apart a bit so the black shows between. Glue two along each side and two across the bottom to make the frame for the picture. Weight it down with a book so it dries flat.

Cut a piece of paper 6 inches wide, 7 inches long. Fold it in half the long way. Draw half a basket on the paper, with the center of the basket and handle along the fold of the paper, as in Fig. 1. Unfold the paper and you will have the whole basket with its curving handle, as in Fig. 2. Use this as a pattern to cut a basket from one of the cloth scraps.

Glue the cloth basket to the black background. Glue pieces of rickrack across the basket below the rim and above the base.

Cut the flowers and leaves from different colors and patterns of cloth scraps, like the ones in Fig. 3—or make up your own.

Arrange the flowers and leaves in the basket. Glue them in place, using glue only at the center of each, so the edges are not tight to the paper.

33

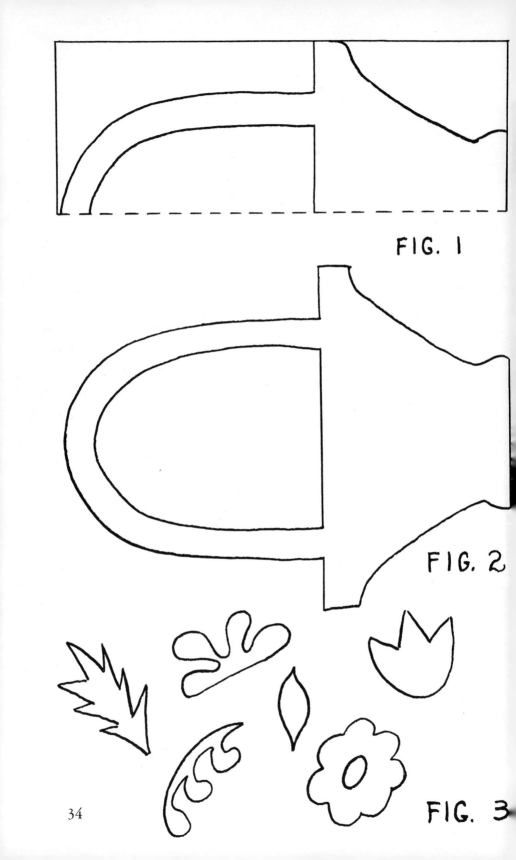

FIG. 1

FIG. 2

FIG. 3

34

PHOTO FRAME

Here's a way to frame a favorite photo. Or you can use a pretty picture cut from a card, a magazine or a calendar, if you wish.

You Will Need:

A 2-pound chocolate drink mix can

Macaroni—the kind that looks like pieces of twisted rope

A photo or picture   White glue   Plastic wrap

Cardboard—the back of a pencil tablet or the lid of a shoebox

Metallic paint—gold, silver or copper (or enamel if you want a colored frame).

How to Make It:

Cut the metal top off the chocolate drink mix can. Take off the lid, you will not need it.

Glue pieces of twisted macaroni around the round opening in the top, and around the edge just inside the rim. Paint the entire frame.

Cut the photo or picture a little larger than the round opening. Cut a piece of clear plastic food wrap the same size as the picture. Lay the wrap and the picture together and fasten at several places with small pieces of scotch tape.

Place the picture behind the opening and tape it to the back of the can top.

Cut the piece of cardboard to the size and shape of Fig. 1.

Lay a ruler along the line XX from A to C. Hold the ruler down tight with one hand and run a knife along the edge to make a crease mark on the cardboard. Do the same with line XX from B to D. Bend the tabs ACE and BDF backwards.

Glue the flat part of the cardboard to the back of the picture frame to make the stand-up easel. Fig. 2 shows the finished frame.

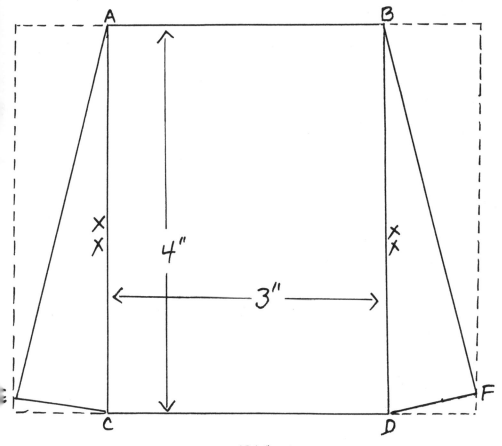

A B

4"

3"

C D F

FIG. 1

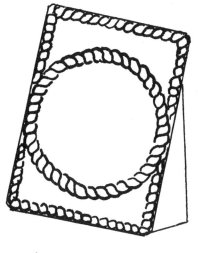

FIG. 2

NESTING-STACKING CANS

Small children like to pile things up or fit one inside the other. Make this set for your little brother or sister, a favorite cousin, or little neighbor.

You Will Need:

Six or eight tin cans that fit inside each other.

Colored pictures from magazine ads

White glue   Gift wrap paper

Clear spray finish—the kind that says "recommended for children's toys and furniture" on the label. Paint stores have it.

How to Make It:

For the largest can use a 3-pound shortening can with a snap-on plastic cover. For the next size use a tall 1-pound coffee can. For the rest, use cans from vegetables and fruits, of different sizes that slip inside each other easily; Fig. 1. Rims of the cans should be very smooth on the inside. Run your fingers around the inside edge and if the rim feels sharp at any point, flatten it by laying the can on the sidewalk or on a wooden block and tapping the sharp place with a hammer.

Cover the cans with gift wrap paper, pulling it smooth and tight.

Look through magazines to find pictures of animals, toys, or others that small children would like. Glue one or two pictures to each can.

After the glue is dry, spray the cans with the clear finish. This will give them a smooth, waterproof coating that can be wiped clean.

When not being played with the cans are placed inside each other and the plastic lid snapped onto the shortening can, to keep them together; Fig. 2.

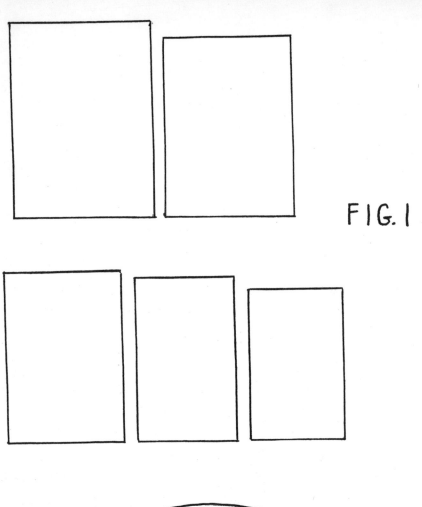

FIG. 1

FIG. 2

LETTER HOLDER

If mom complains that the letters are always getting mislaid before she can answer them, she'll like this letter holder with three compartments to keep track of her mail.

You Will Need:

Three square paper plates

Heavy colored crochet thread or carpet warp

A paper punch

White glue

How to Make It:

Cut each of the paper plates in half.

Lay the two halves of a plate together, top side in, and glue the halves together around the rim to make a "pocket," as in Fig. 1.

Punch holes 1/4 inch in from the edge, 1/2 inch apart, all around the rim.

Lace around the rim with a piece of thread, beginning at one end, around to the other. Then lace back the other way, so the lacing crosses the first row, around the edge of the plate, as in Fig. 2.

Glue the edges together, punch and lace the other two plates in the same way.

Glue the flat parts of the three "pockets" together, with the bottom edges even. Hold the "pockets" together where they are glued at the top edges, with spring clothespins, until the glue is dry. Set the letter holder on a table to dry, so the bottom edges will stay in line.

Write or print the word "MAIL" or "LETTERS" on one side of the letter holder.

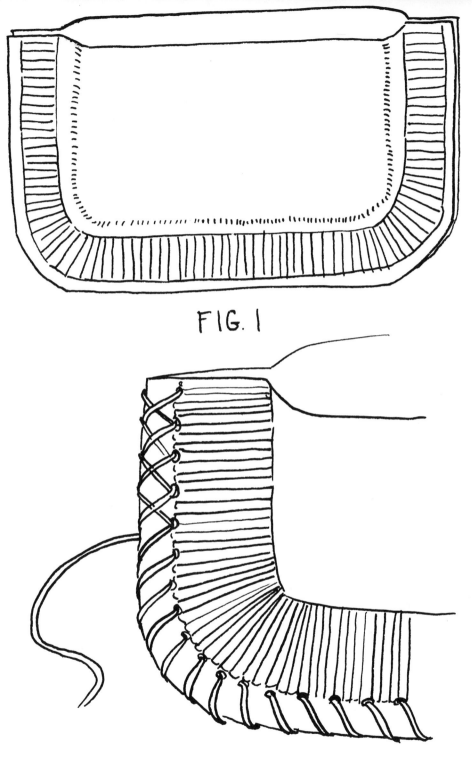

FIG. 1

FIG. 2

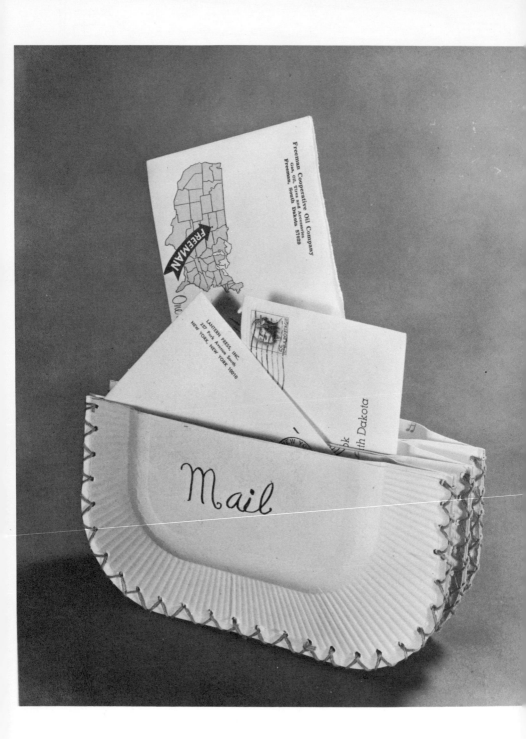

BATHTUB SCRUBBER

This handy little gadget makes it easy to get rid of the "ring around the tub" when the bathwater gurgles down the drain.

You Will Need:

Nylon net

Grosgrain ribbon,—1 inch wide, 8 inches long

String or heavy crochet thread

Thread and needle

How to Make It:

Cut the nylon net into strips 2 inches wide, 5 inches long.

Cut a piece of string 30 inches long and double it through the center. Cut another piece of string about 15 inches long. Slip it through the loop made by the center of the doubled string and tie it to a chair back or doorknob, Fig. 1.

Hold the doubled string apart between the thumb and fingers of your left hand. Lay a strip of net across the two strings. Bring the ends of the net down on the outsides of the doubled string, under and up inside the doubled string. Push the knotted strand to the end of the doubled string, Fig. 2.

Keep adding strips until the 15 inch long doubled string is filled.

Tie the ends of the string together in a square knot to keep the net from slipping off. Untie and pull out the short piece of string tied to the chair back.

Fold one end of the strand back against itself for about 3 inches. Sew the knotted net together. Keep wrapping and sewing the strand around and around, as in Fig. 3.

Lap the ends of the grosgrain ribbon for 1 inch and sew them together. Sew the ribbon to the knotted coil of the nylon scrubber to make the handle, Fig. 4.

The ends of the net strips fan out to make a fluffy ruffle.
Slip your hand through the handle, as in the photo, to use.

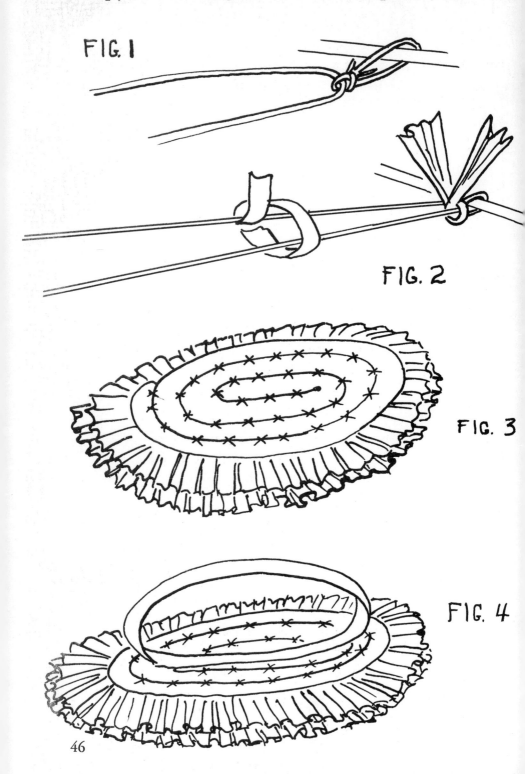

FIG. I

FIG. 2

FIG. 3

FIG. 4

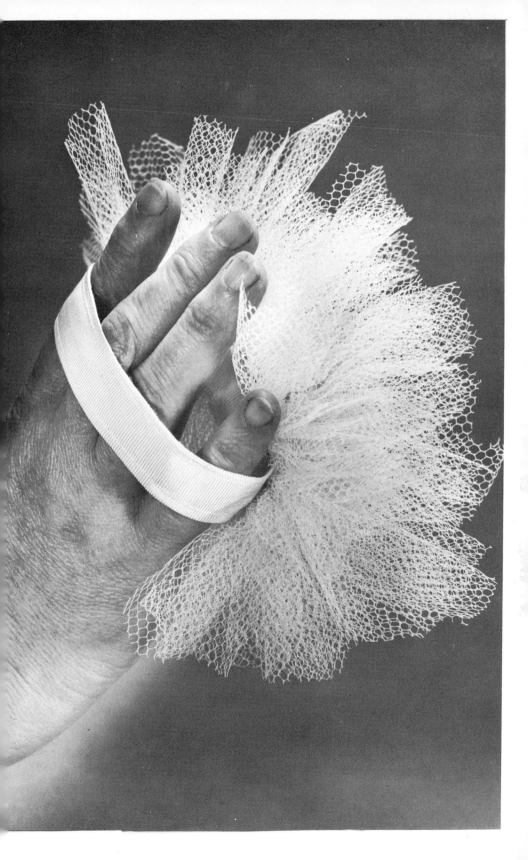

SPRING BONNET PINCUSHION

Using a pin to hold a hat is the accepted thing, but here's a hat that holds pins. Easy to make and nice to use or give as a gift.

You Will Need:

A plastic doily—5 or 6 inches diameter

A scrap of cloth   Needle and thread   Steel wool

The core tube from a role of waxed paper or paper towels

Ribbon—12 inches long   A small cloth or plastic flower

How to Make It:

Cut a 1 1/4 inch section from the end of the paper tube. This will be the crown of the hat.

Fill the center of the tubing section with steel wool, Fig. 1.

Cut a 5 inch diameter circle. Make a line of running stitches around the circle 1/4 inch from the edge. Lay the steel wool filled tubing section in the center of the cloth section and draw up the line of stitching to gather the cloth circle around the tubing. Pull the cover of the hat crown tight and take a few knotting stitches to keep it in place. Clip the thread. Fig. 2 shows the gathering.

Set the hat crown onto the center of the plastic doily and fasten it in place with stitches through the cloth at the edge of the crown and around the ribs of the doily, Fig. 3.

Add the ribbon around the crown where it is sewed to the doily, cross the ends and catch with several stitches where they cross.

Tack the flower in place at the cross point of the ribbon to finish it.

48

FIG. 1

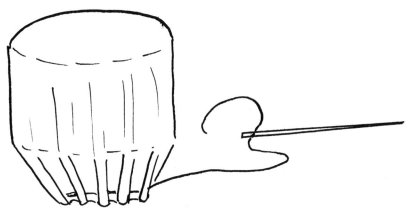

FIG. 2

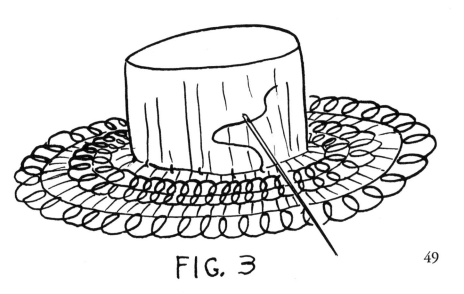

FIG. 3

49

SHADE PULL

It's easier to pull down the window shade when you have a "handle" to take hold of.

You Will Need:

Two plastic detergent bottle caps

Two matching small buttons,—3/8 inch or 1/2 inch in diameter

One large button,—1 1/4 inch to 1 1/2 inch in diameter

Colored carpet warp or heavy crochet thread

Cardboard,—2 inches wide, 3 inches long

How to Make It:

Cut a piece of carpet warp or crochet thread 12 inches long. Double it at the center and tie the end into a knot, leaving a loop about 1 inch long above the knot.

Pass the two ends of the thread through the two holes of a small button. Push the button against the knot.

Roll the two ends of the thread together and pass them through the hole in a detergent bottle cap where it was snipped off.

Pass the two ends of the thread through the two holes in the large button, then through the hole in the second bottle cap, from the inside to the outside.

Again pass the two thread ends through the holes in the second small button. Fig. 1 shows how the parts are strung together. Push the parts against each other and tie the thread ends into a square knot against the second small button to hold the parts tight together.

Wrap thread around the cardboard, taking about 18 turns around the card.

Slip a short piece of thread behind the wrapped strands against the cardboard at one end and tie it into a square knot to hold the threads together, Fig. 2.

Clip the threads where they pass around the other end of the cardboard.

Tie a thread around the tassel about 1/2 inch below the knotted top, Fig. 3.

Trim the bottoms of the threads even and tie the tassel to the bottom of the curtain pull.

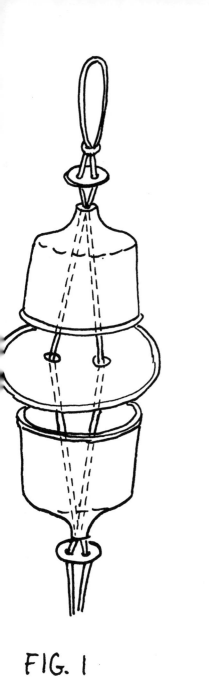

FIG. 1

FIG. 2

FIG. 3.

PILL BOTTLE BUD VASE

This glittery little vase is just right for a single rosebud or other flower. It makes a nice tray favor for someone who is ill.

You Will Need:

A straight-sided pill bottle that has a snap-on plastic cover instead of a screw-on lid.

A small piece of light cardboard—from a pencil tablet back or cereal box.   White glue   Gold glitter

How to Make It:

Cut a cardboard circle a little larger than the diameter of the bottle. Our bottle measures 1 inch in diameter, so we cut the cardboard circle 1 1/4 inch in diameter.

Glue the cardboard circle to the bottom of the pill bottle, being careful to set the bottle in the center of the circle as in Fig. 1. Set the bottle on its base aside to dry before you do any more work on it.

When the glue is dry, spread a sheet of waxed paper on the table. Work over it when putting the glitter on the vase. Some of the glitter will fall off and it can be poured back into the container from the paper.

Spread white glue over part of the bottle. Be sure the glue is evenly spread. Sprinkle glitter on the bottle. It will stick to the glue. Spread glue on another part of the bottle and sprinkle on more glitter. Cover the entire bottle and the top of the cardboard base. Shake off any loose glitter.

After the glue has dried, examine the vase for any thin spots that are not covered with glitter. Spread on glue again and sprinkle on glitter, to make an all-over even coat with no glass or cardboard showing through.

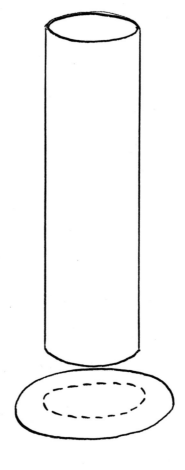

FIG. 1

MADAME WHISK

With a swish of her skirts, Madame Whisk removes the lint from your clothes. Of course, you have to make her skirts swish, but she doesn't mind at all having you hold her by the head to do it.

You Will Need:

Art Foam (buy it at a craft shop or order from a hobby supply catalogue)

Three empty thread spools, one a bit larger than the other two

A 7 inch long dowel, thin enough to slip through the holes in the spools but not fit too loosely

Hobby enamels

Clear fingernail polish

Black embroidery thread

Pinking shears

White glue

How to Make It:

For the skirt, cut a piece of art foam 5 inches wide, 36 inches long.

Fold the piece in half, lengthwise, Fig. 1. Hold it together with the edges even while you snip with the pinking shears from the folded edge to within 1/2 inch of the cut edges. Make the snips 1/2 inch apart and clip the entire length of the doubled piece, Fig. 2.

Spread glue between the two thicknesses of foam between the uncut portions of the doubled strip. Spread glue around the dowel at one end for about 2 inches. Wrap the uncut portion of the strip around the end of the dowel, the cut part extending beyond the end. Pull the foam tight and wrap spirally along the dowel with each turn around the dowel just a bit beyond the one before. When you reach the end of the glue covered portion of the dowel, spread on more glue and continue wrapping, Fig. 3, until all of the strip has been wrapped around the dowel. Tie string around the end of the foam to hold it tight against the dowel until the glue dries. The dowel left uncovered with foam should be as long as the combined height of the three spools.

For the hat, cut two circles of foam 1 1/2 inch in diameter. Lay one circle on top of the other. Thread an embroidery needle with black embroidery thread. Run a circle of stitching about 3/4 inch in diameter, leaving 1 inch of the end of the thread hanging free. When you have stitched all the way around, through the two thicknesses of foam, hold both ends of the thread and pull them tight to make the center puff up into a crown and the brim wavy. Tie the ends of the thread together in a square knot. Leave about 1/2 inch of threads beyond the knot for the "ribbon." Fig. 4 and 5 show how the hat is made.

Paint the two spools for the body with hobby enamels, any color you wish. Two coats will be needed for a smooth finish. Coat the larger head spool with clear nail polish. When it is dry, paint on the hair and features with hobby enamels, as in Fig. 6.

Spread glue on the rest of the dowel. Slip on a body spool. Spread glue on the end of the spool and slip on the second spool. Spread glue on its end and slip on the head spool, Fig. 7.

Spread glue on the end of the head spool and set the hat on top of her head.

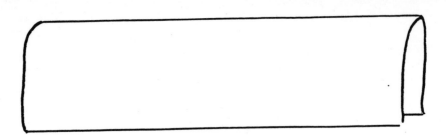

FIG. 1

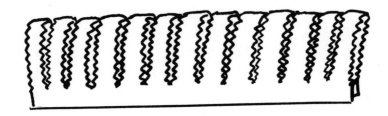

FIG. 2

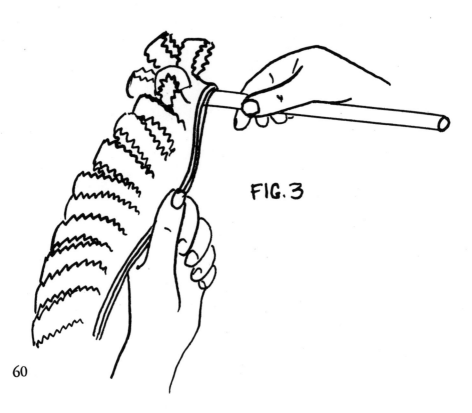

FIG. 3

FIG. 4

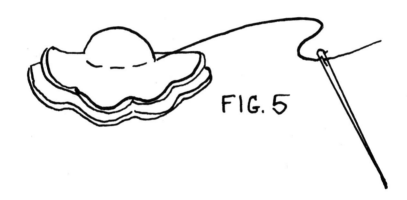

FIG. 5

FIG. 6

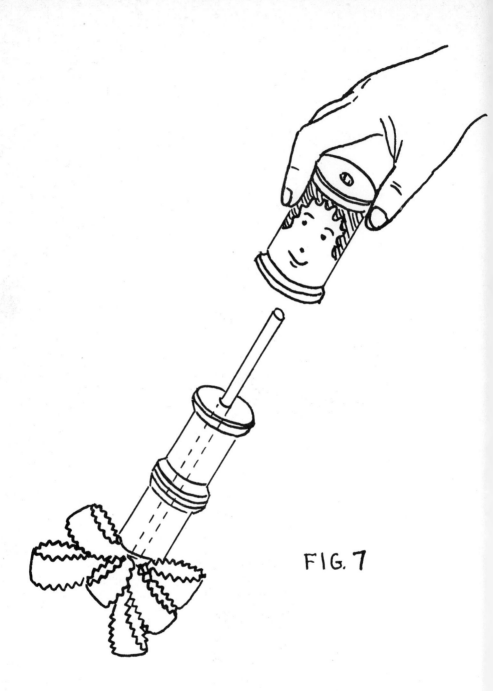

FIG. 7

BIRDCAGE FLOWER HOLDER

Instead of a bird, this miniature cage holds artificial flowers. It is a pretty decoration hanging from a wall bracket or in a window.

You Will Need:

Plastic drinking straws

White "pearl cotton" thread

A needle with a large eye

Plastic flowers—sweet peas or other "vining'" flowers or greenery

How to Make It:

Cut 9 drinking straws in half for the 18 ribs of the cage.

Cut 9 pieces of straw, each 1 inch long, for the spreaders between the ribs.

Thread the needle with a piece of pearl cotton. Tie a knot in the thread about 2 inches from the end.

Push the needle through one of the rib pieces, 1/4 inch from the end of the straw. Pull the thread through until the knot is against the rib.

Push the needle through a second rib and pull the thread through until the two ribs are together, one pointing up, the other down.

Thread the needle through one of the spreader pieces. Push the spreader along the thread until it is against the rib.

Push the needle through two more ribs, then thread through a spreader, and so on until all ribs and spreaders are on the thread. Fig. 1 shows how this is done.

Tie the ends of the thread together in a square knot and clip off the extra thread.

Thread the needle again and tie a knot about 2 inches from the end.

Push the needle through the ends of all the straws that point up. Pull the thread tight and tie it in a square knot. This brings the cage ribs together into a point at the top, as shown in Fig. 2. Clip off the extra thread.

Gather the bottom ribs together in the same way.

Make a tassel of pearl cotton, following the directions given for the shade pull tassel. Tie the tassel to the bottom of the cage.

Tuck the flowers between the ribs so that some of them hang out and down.

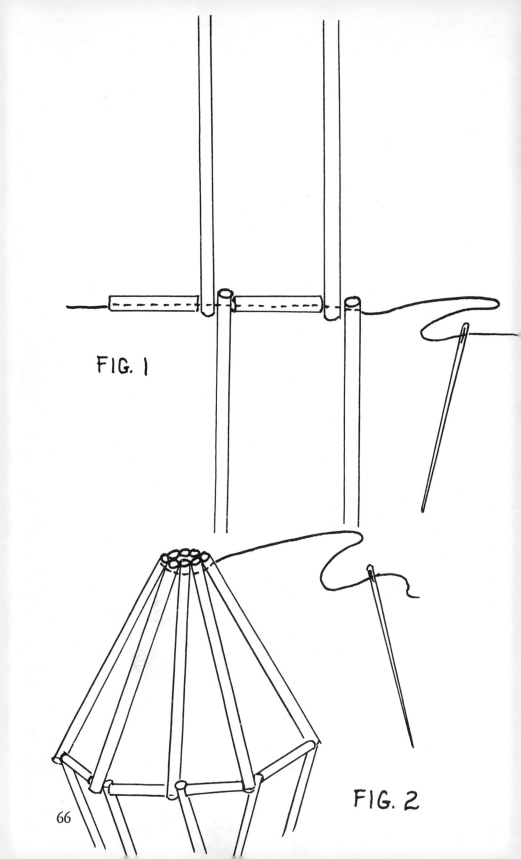

FIG. 1

FIG. 2

RIBBON ROSE CORSAGE

This corsage won't wilt like one of fresh flowers, so it can be used over and over again.

You Will Need:

1 1/2 inch wide ribbon, 24 inches long—for the large rose

1 inch wide ribbon, 24 inches long—two pieces, for the small roses

1/2 inch wide ribbon, 2 yards long—for the bow

Plastic fern

Needle and thread

How to Make It:

For the rose, make a right angle fold in the center of the piece of ribbon, as shown in Fig. 1.

Bring end A back over end B, as in Fig. 2.

Bring end B up over A, as in Fig. 3, then A back over B, then B down over A—and continue folding the ribbon ends over each other to the ends of the ribbon, as in Fig. 4.

Hold the ends to keep from unfolding and release the stack of folds. It will look like Fig. 5.

Hold one end of the ribbon and pull down slowly on the other end. The ribbon will telescope into itself. Pull the free end of the ribbon until the first fold almost disappears in the center of the flower, Fig. 6.

Now the folds of ribbon resemble the petals of a rose. Stitch the ribbon tightly together at the base of the rose, and cut off the extra ribbon you pulled down.

Make the two other roses the same way.

Cut a piece of plastic fern about 6 inches long. Arrange the roses on the fern, and catch them to it with several stitches.

Arrange the ribbon for the bow by folding it back and forth in 4 inch long loops—Fig. 7.

Tie the loops together at the center—Fig. 8—leaving the ends of the tying ribbon long enough to tie the ribbon bow to the fern.

Spread and fluff out the bow before tying it to the corsage.

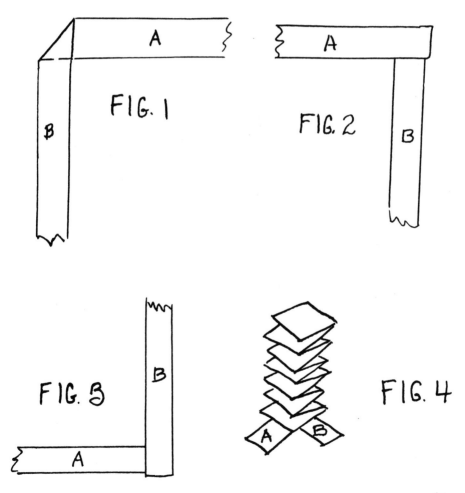

FIG. 1

FIG. 2

FIG. 3

FIG. 4

FIG. 5

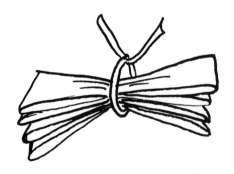

FIG. 6

FIG. 7

FIG. 8

TINY VASES

These miniature vases are just the right size to hold bouquets of small flowers such as violets, pansies, or a single rosebud with a few leaves.

You Will Need:

Eggshells   Darning needle   Hobby enamels
Construction paper   White glue   Toothpicks

How to Make It:

When mother is cooking scrambled eggs, ask her to let you empty the shells. Instead of cracking them in the usual way, do it like this. Punch a hole through the pointed end of the shell with the darning needle. Use the needle to break away a little of the shell at a time around the hole until the opening measures about 3/4 inch across, Fig. 1.

Turn the egg upside down over a bowl and shake out the white and yolk.

Rinse out the eggshells and turn them upside down in a pan to dry.

When the inside is dry, paint the outsides of the shells with your hobby enamels. Leave them just one color or decorate them by painting a design on one side.

Make the base from construction paper of a color that matches or contrasts with the painted shell. Draw a circle 2 inches in diameter. Inside it, draw another circle 1 1/2 inch in diameter. Mark off one-fourth of the circle and inside the rest draw points, as shown in Fig. 2.

Cut out the three-fourths of the circle and points. Lap and glue the ends together and fold the points outward, Fig. 2.

Spread glue on the insides of the points and set the eggshell on the base. Press the points against the shell.

For the handles, cut two strips of construction paper each 1/4 inch wide, 2 1/2 inches long. Roll the ends around a toothpick and shape the handle as shown in Fig. 3.

Glue the handles to the sides of the vase, Fig. 4.

If you want a single basket handle, cut a strip 1/4 inch wide, 9 inches long. Glue the ends to the base points at opposite sides of the shell, with the handle curving over the top.

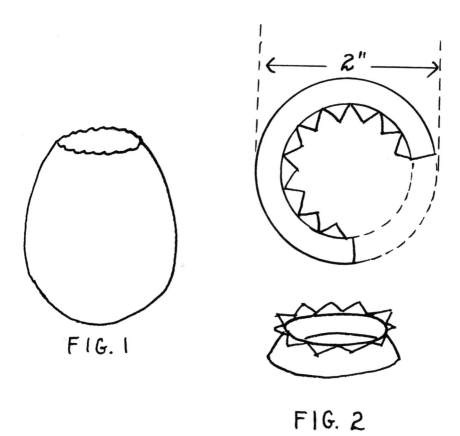

FIG. 1

FIG. 2

HANDLE STRIP

2 ½" LONG, ¼" WIDE

FIG. 3

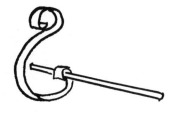

FIG. 4

MAGICAL UNDERSEA GARDEN

Your friends will think you are a magician when they see your undersea garden with "snowballs" bouncing up and down.

You Will Need:

A small goldfish bowl or glass jar

Mothballs

Baking soda

A handful of pebbles or pearl chips

Artificial goldfish and plastic plants used for aquariums

White vinegar

Baking soda

Water

How to Make It:

Place the pebbles in the bottom of the bowl. Add the plants, fish and half a dozen mothballs.

Mix the magic solution. Use one part vinegar and three parts water, plus 1/2 teaspoonful of soda for each cupful of solution. If your bowl holds one quart, use 1 cup of vinegar, 3 cups water and 2 teaspoons of baking soda.

Pour the solution slowly into the bowl. Bubbles from the fizzing liquid gather on the mothballs and soon they will rise to the top, stay up for a little while then drop back to the bottom to gather more bubbles and rise again. They will keep bobbing for a long time.

When the "fizz" wears out, just add more soda to make the balls bob again.

TAN'S PICTURE PUZZLE CARDS

About 2,000 years ago,—so we've been told—a Chinese gentleman named Mr. Tan got bored. He had too much free time and didn't know what to do with it. He invented a set of picture puzzle cards and spent hours arranging them into all sorts of pictures. Why don't you try it?

You Will Need:

> Black cardboard—about the weight of a pencil tablet back   Ruler   Pencil   Scissors

How to Make It:

Draw a square on the cardboard. Any size may be used but six inch sides are a good size to work with. Draw a diagonal line from C to B (see diagram). Make a mark halfway between A and B, and a mark halfway between A and C. Draw the line FG. Make a mark at the center of FG and draw a line from it to the corner D to get JD. Make a mark halfway between E and B on the line CB. Draw the line GH. Make a mark halfway between E and C, and draw the line JK. Cut along the lines to make the seven pieces.

Arrange the cards to make a picture. Try the man with the rice bowl. Take away the rice bowl and turn it to a different position at the bottom of the robe and you have a man making a speech. The fish is another easy one, so is the cat. In the photograph we turn the cat into a dog by changing the arrangement of some of the pieces.

There are only two "rules" for using Tan's picture puzzle cards: all seven pieces must be used in making a single picture, and each piece must be completely seen. That is, the cards may not be arranged with one piece partly covering another. You may use the cards either side up, however. For this reason it is best to use cardboard black on both sides.

Pictures of the rickshaw man, the lady and baby carriage, the race, and the wrestlers are made of two sets of cards, one set used for each figure.

These picture puzzle cards make a fine game when several friends come to visit. Make a set for each person.

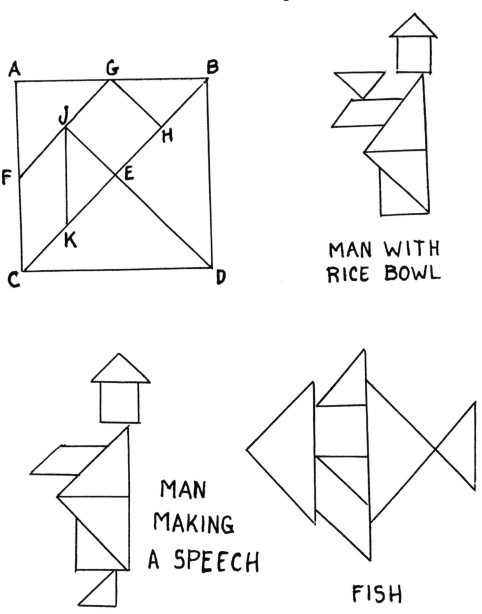

MAN WITH
RICE BOWL

MAN
MAKING
A SPEECH

FISH

LADY WITH BABY
CARRIAGE

THE RACE

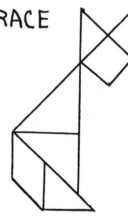

CAT

RICKSHAW MAN

80

WRESTLERS

BUTTERFLIES

Have you ever wished you could keep a butterfly for a pet? You can't do that with a live one, of course, but these look almost as pretty as real ones on your curtains.

You Will Need:

Crepe paper—yellow, pink, or whatever you wish the wings to be.

Doll clothespins   Gold glitter   White glue

Florist's wire or fine spool wire   Sequins, tiny beads

How to Make It:

Cut a piece of crepe paper 4 inches by 6 inches for each butterfly. The grain of the paper should run crosswise.

Cut the piece of paper to the shape of butterfly wings as shown in Fig. 1.

Cut a piece of wire 5 inches long. Wrap the center of the wire around the base of the clothespin knob, twist together. Thread a bead on each end and bend the wire back to keep the bead in place. Point the wires up to make the butterfly feelers. See Fig. 2.

Wrap a short piece of wire around one prong of the clothespin against the crotch. Twist the ends together and point the wire downward, Fig. 2. This wire is used to "pin" the butterfly to the curtain by slipping it between the threads.

With the point of a paring knife spread glue between the prongs.

82

Work the center of the wings up into the crotch of the clothespin, pushing the paper into tight gathers as in Fig. 3. The prongs of the pin should be 1/2 inch below the paper when it is all gathered. Spread and shape the wings.

Spread a line of glue along the edge of the wings and sprinkle on gold glitter.

Glue colored sequins to the wings for spots.

Glue two gold sequins to the clothespin knob to make eyes. Glue two tiny black beads to the centers of the sequins for pupils.

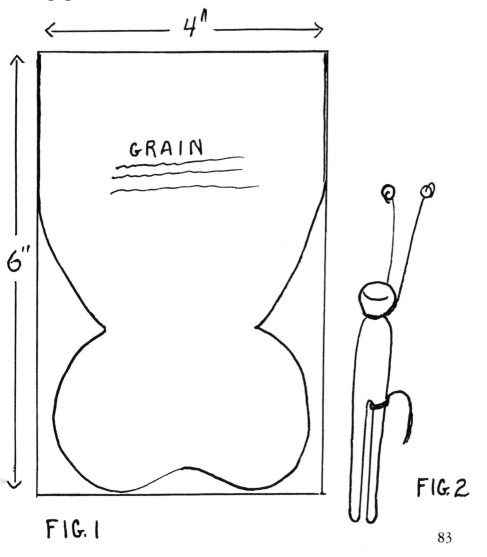

4"

6"

GRAIN

FIG. 1

FIG. 2

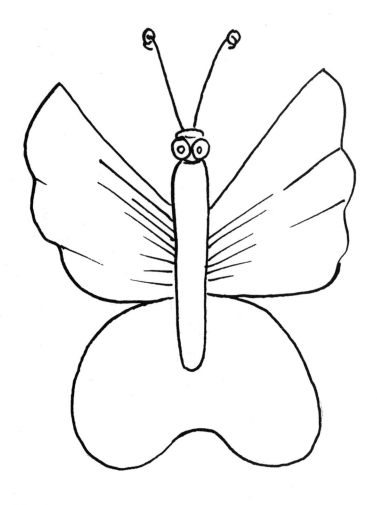

FIG. 3

FANNY SOAP-FISH

Fanny is a "fun" present for you to make.

You Will Need:

A bar of soap that is oval in shape (Sweetheart or Dove)

Nylon net (green or orange for a "goldfish")

Ribbon—3/4 inch wide

Sequins

Straight pins

Black construction paper

How to Make It:

Cut a piece of nylon net 12 inches square. Place one point of the oval of the bar of soap down onto the center of the net. Gather the net around the bar of soap, holding it tight around the other point of the oval.

Wrap thread around the gathers and tie tightly to hold them together.

Spread the net beyond the tie to make the tail.

Cut six pieces of ribbon, each 2 inches long.

Bring the ends of a piece of ribbon forward and down, crossing them as in Fig. 1 to make a cone shape.

Place the crossed portion of the cone against the under side of the body, near the tail. Push a pin through the ribbon and into the bar of soap to hold the bottom fin in place. Pin a second ribbon cone ahead of the first to complete the bottom fin.

Use three ribbon cones to make the upper fin, pinning them on from the back to the front, pulling one over the other as shown in fig. 2.

Pin a single cone to the front of the body to make the fin just behind the gill. Push the pin in at a slant so the pin does not stick through the bar.

Cut a thin curving piece from black construction paper to make the gill line. Push the points through the opening in the mesh to hold the "gill" in place. Fig. 2 shows this.

Pin on a black sequin for the eye, and several more colored ones to make the spots on the back, as shown in Fig. 2.

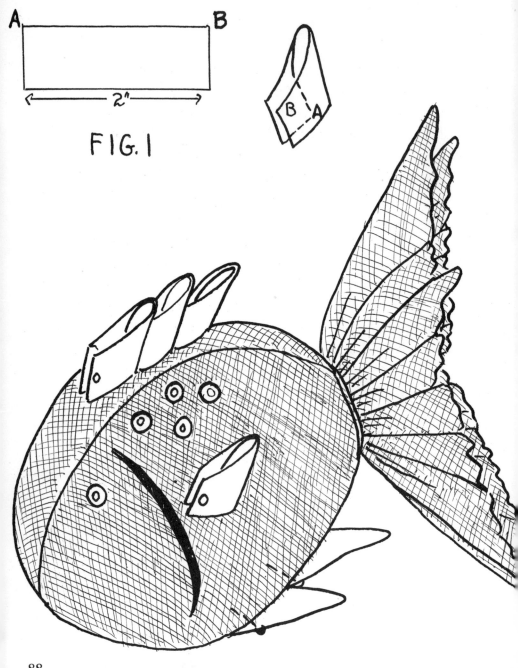

A   B

2"

FIG. 1

B   A

FIG. 2

DOLL CLOTHES

Do you sew for your dolls? Here's an easy way to make a knitted suit and cap set for a small boy doll.

You Will Need:

> Three cuffs from worn out socks—the cuffs are usually
> still good even though there are holes in the heels or
> toes of the socks.
>
> Scraps of yarn
>
> Needle, and thread matching the color of the socks.

How to Make It:

Cut the cuffs off the socks. One cuff makes the pants, one the slip-over sleeveless sweater, and the third becomes the stocking cap.

For the sweater—use the top of the cuff as the top of the sweater. Turn the top back about 1/2 inch to make the "turtle neck." Lay the double cuff flat. About 1/2 inch below the top cut small, half-circle openings for the armholes, as in Fig. 1. because these openings are cut on the fold of the sock, they are really round holes for the arms.

Fold over the bottom edge twice to turn under the cut edge of the cuff and make the bottom of the sweater.

For the pants—use the top of the cuff for the bottom of the pant legs. Lay the double cuff down flat. Sew the two thicknesses together for about 1/2 inch at the center, as shown in Fig. 2. If the pants are too long on top, cut them off so they are the right length to come to the doll's waist.

For the cap—use the top of the cuff for the bottom of the cap. Gather the cut end of the cuff by running a line of stitches all around, about 1/4 inch from the edge. Draw the thread tight and fasten, to gather shut the top of the cap, Fig. 3. Turn inside out so the gathered edge is on the inside top of the cap.

Make the pompom for the top of the cap from scraps of yarn. Cut a piece of light cardboard 1 inch wide, 1 1/2 inch long. Wrap yarn around width of the cardboard for 20 turns. Slip a piece of yarn behind the yarn against the cardboard, along one edge. Tie the ends of the yarn tightly together in a square knot, to hold the strands of yarn together, Fig. 4. Clip the strands of yarn where they pass around the other edge of the cardboard. The strands will puff out into a pompom. Sew it to the top of the cap.

Turn back the bottom of the cap just as you roll your own stocking cap.

SWEATER, FIG. 1

PANTS, FIG. 2

CAP, FIG. 3

FIG. 4

91

CLOWN DOOR STOP

Clancy, the clown, smiles happily as he keeps the door from banging.

You Will Need:

    A one-quart syrup bottle

    Felt—red and black

    Cloth—for his suit

    Rug yarn for hair and pompoms

    An old nylon stocking

    The toe of a white sock

    Sand

    Thread and needle

How to Make It:

Wash and dry the bottle. Fill it with sand and screw on the cap.

Cut a circle of cloth, 18 inches in diameter. Lay it on the table, wrong side up. Set the bottle in the center of the circle. Bring the cloth up around the bottle and wrap string tightly around the top of the bottle. Tie in a square knot to hold the cloth in place.

Cut off the sock about halfway between the toe and heel. Stuff the toe with nylon stocking. Slip the opening down onto the neck of the bottle as in Fig. 1. Tie a string tightly around the neck, Fig. 2.

93

Cut the eyes, nose and mouth from red felt and glue the pieces to the face.

Cut short strands of rug yarn (any color you choose) and sew them to the head for hair. Fig. 2 shows the features and hair added to the head.

Make a paper pattern for the hat. Draw a 3 inch diameter circle. Cut it into three pieces. Use one of the pieces as a pattern and cut the cap from red felt, Fig. 3. Roll the felt into a cone and glue or sew the edges together. Glue the hat to Clancy's head between the tufts of hair.

Make a paper pattern for the collar from an envelope, cutting it double. Unfold the pattern and cut the collar from red felt. Fit the collar around Clancy's neck. Glue or stitch the lapped ends.

Make two yarn pompoms following the directions given for the doll stocking cap pompom. Sew them to the front of the suit.

Cut two feet from black felt using the pattern in Fig. 4. Glue them to the bottom of the doorstop.

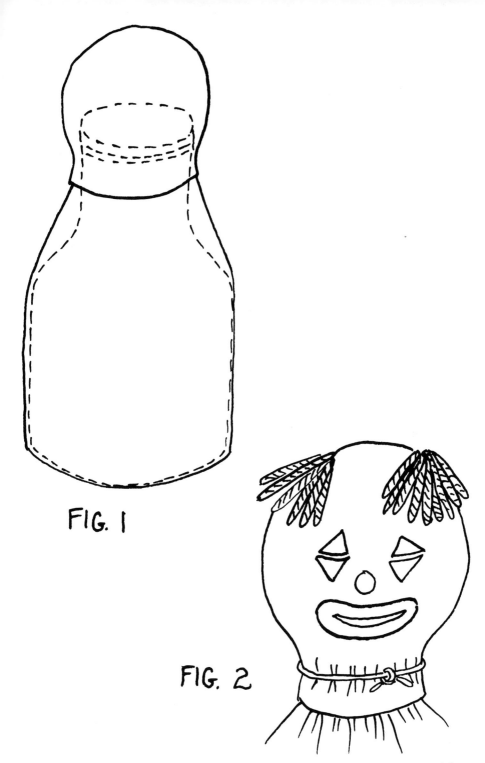

FIG. 1

FIG. 2

95

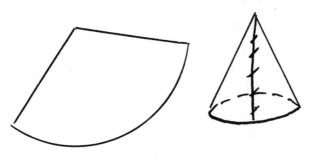

FIG. 3

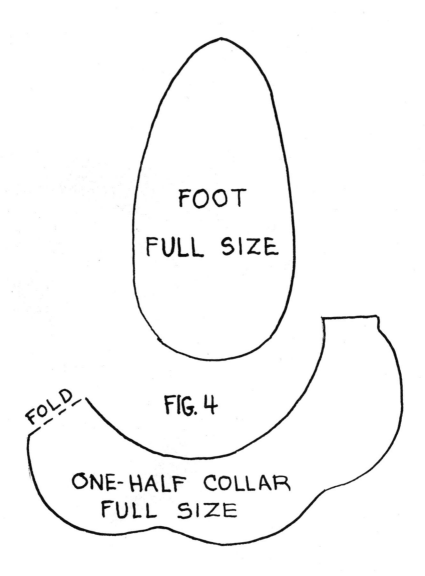

FOOT
FULL SIZE

FOLD

FIG. 4

ONE-HALF COLLAR
FULL SIZE

GOLDFISH BOWL FLOATERS

A sailboat or a turtle makes an interesting addition to your aquarium. Your little brother will probably want to borrow them for bathtub toys.

You Will Need:

For the sailboat

A thermos bottle cork

The burr from a bolt—measuring about 3/4 inch across

A flathead screw—1 inch long

Typing paper

2 round toothpicks

Glue

For the turtle

A green candle end

Half a walnut shell

A clean tin can

How to Make It:

The boat. Pass the screw through the hole in the burr and screw the point up into the cork to make it float upright, Fig. 1.

Cut two sails and a flag from typing paper. Punch small holes through the sails near the top and bottom, as shown in Fig. 2. Paint the flag.

Curve the sails and slip a toothpick mast through the holes in each, Fig. 3. Glue the flag to the mast of the larger sail. Break off about 1/4 inch of the top of the mast on the smaller sail.

Use a darning needle to poke two holes into the top of the cork. Push the ends of the toothpick masts into the holes.

The turtle. Shave the green candle end into the tin can. Set the can into a pan of hot water. When the wax is melted take the pan out of the hot water and let the wax cool until it is thickened but not hard. Pick up some of the wax and work it with your fingers. You can mold it just like modeling clay. Shape the head and press the neck against the round end of the shell. Shape the feet and press them in place. The pointed end of the shell makes the tail.

Fill the rest of the shell with soft wax to make the under side of the turtle. If the wax hardens before you finish, set the can in hot water to soften the wax again.

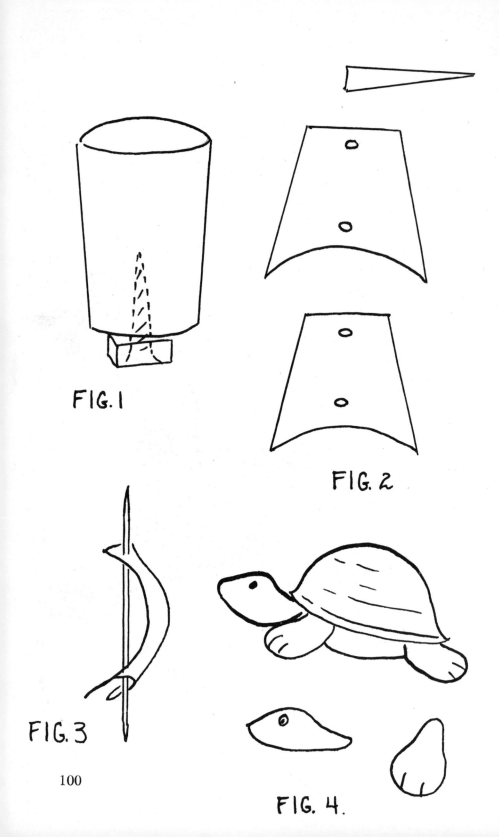

FIG. 1

FIG. 2

FIG. 3

FIG. 4.

CLIMBING BUTTONS

Whoever heard of buttons that climb a string? These do. With practice you can make them do all sorts of tricks.

You Will Need:

Two large overcoat buttons with four holes and rounded backs

A button that measures about 3/4 inch across

Heavy thread—24 inches long

Needle and thread

How to Make It:

Sew the two large buttons together, back to back, Fig. 1.

Tie one end of the thread tightly around the threads holding the buttons together.

Tie the small button to the other end of the thread.

Wrap the thread around the center between the two buttons, Fig. 2.

Hold the small button in your hand and let the large ones drop. They will run down the string and back up again.

At first you may have trouble making them come all the way back up but as you practice you will learn how to give the string just the right "twitch" to keep the buttons going up and down.

When you have learned how to do this, try throwing the buttons straight out in front of you and back. This is more difficult but it can be done.

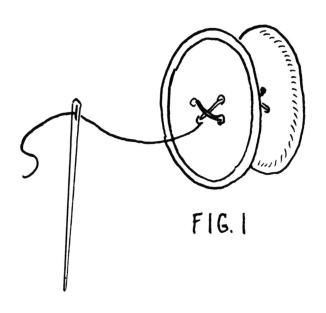

FIG. 1

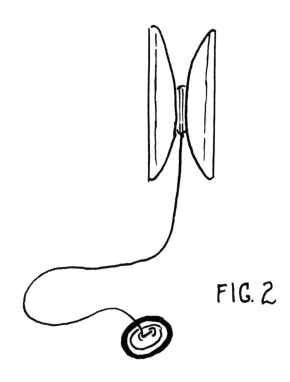

FIG. 2

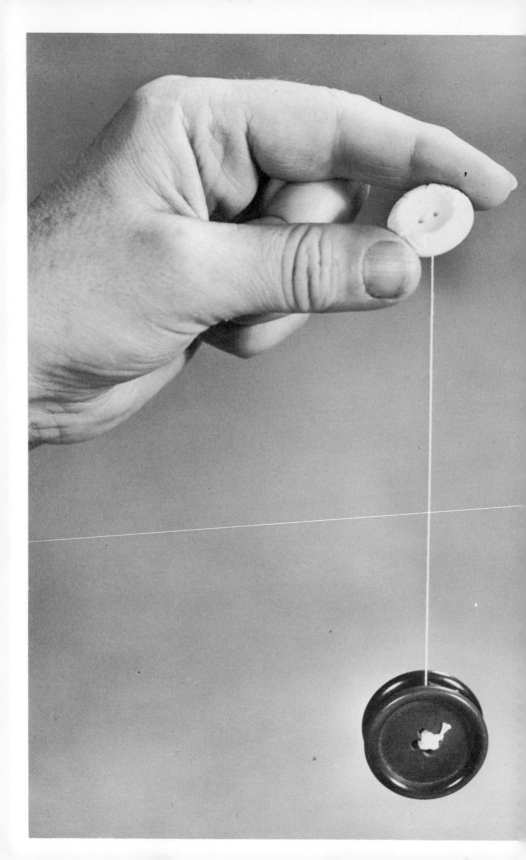

FLOWERING SPRING BRANCH

In many parts of the country, spring, with its flowering trees and shrubs, is a long time coming. When the trees finally do have clouds of pink and white blossoms, they last only a few days. By assisting Nature a bit, you can have a blossoming apple branch to decorate your wall as early in spring, and as long as you wish. The branch is real but the blossoms are "made by you."

You Will Need:

A branch about 4 feet long, or the right size to fit your wall space.

Duplex crepe paper, white on one side, pink on the other (you can glue pink and white crepe paper together instead)

Crepe paper—green, yellow

Fine flower wire

Small artificial birds—the kind used for dressing up potted plants

Glue

How to Make It:

Cut a strip of crepe paper petals for each blossom like Fig. 1. The grain of the paper should run up and down the petals.

For centers cut a piece of yellow crepe paper 1 inch wide, 1 inch long. Clip into a fine fringe 1/2 inch deep, with the grain, for each blossom.

Gather the unclipped part of the yellow paper into a tight bunch.

Gather the strip of petals around the center, with the white to the outside.

Wrap wire tightly around the gathered portion. Twist the ends of the wire together into a stem about 1 inch below the petals.

Cut a strip of green crepe paper 1/2 inch wide across the entire fold of crepe paper. Beginning just below the petals, wrap the gathered portion and the wire with green crepe paper. Cut off and glue the end.

Make more blossoms the same way, Fig. 2.

Buds—Roll a little piece of crepe paper into a tight ball about 1/4 inch across. Cut a 1 1/4 inch square of pink crepe paper. Place the ball in the center and bring the paper around it. Fig. 3. Twist the paper tightly below the ball. Wrap the twisted part with wire then with green crepe paper as you did the blossoms, to look like Fig. 4.

Cut leaves from green crepe paper the shape shown in Fig. 5, with the grain running lengthwise. Twist the long tongue below the leaf into a stem.

To assemble a bunch of blossoms, hold the stems of two buds and three blossoms together and twist for about 1/2 inch from the bottom. Add two leaves where the stems of the buds and blossoms come together and wrap the entire bunch with green crepe paper.

Prepare as many bunches of blossoms, buds and leaves as you need for your branch. Glue the bunches to the branch where they would naturally come out.

Wire one or two little birds to the branch to add life and color.

You can hang the flowering branch flat against the wall or make a small one to put into a vase.

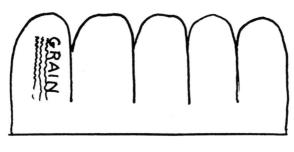

FIG. 1

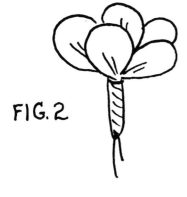

FIG. 2

FIG. 3

FIG. 4

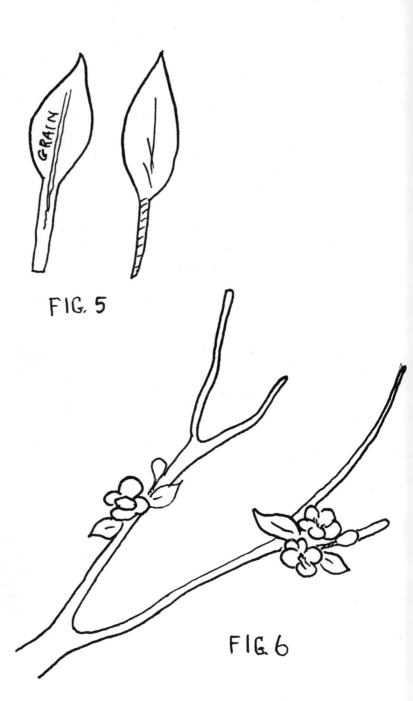

FIG. 5

FIG. 6

BALANCING BUSTER

Buster is a talented acrobat who swings and sways and twirls, bobbing back and forth on his pop bottle stunt stand, without falling off.

You Will Need:

Three detergent bottle caps with "snip off" tips.

Two pipe cleaners   Construction paper

A 1 inch diameter styrofoam ball   White glue

How to Make It:

Two of the bottle caps may have their tips snipped off but the third should still have its little round knob as it came from the store.

Bend back 1/4 inch at one end of a pipe cleaner. Slip the other end of the pipe cleaner through the hole in the tip of the cap, from the inside to the outside. Slide the cap all the way down against the bent back portion of the pipe cleaner, Fig. 1. Prepare the second pipe cleaner and cap in the same way.

Hold the free ends of the pipe cleaners together, side by side, and twist for about 3/4 inch. Curve the pipe cleaners out and down, Fig. 2.

Fill the tip of the third cap with glue and push the twisted ends of the pipe cleaners down into the tip and the curved part resting on the edge, Fig. 3.

Cut eyes, nose and mouth from construction paper and glue them to the styrofoam ball. Make a cone from half a 3/4 inch diameter circle for a hat. Cut a bow tie from paper. Glue the hat to the top of the head.

Glue the head to the cap, then the necktie in place to the front of the ball and cap, hiding the pipe cleaners.

Set Buster on a capped bottle. You may have to bend the pipe cleaners to get them adjusted just right so he will balance.

Twirl him, tap him. He'll bob and sway and turn but not fall off.

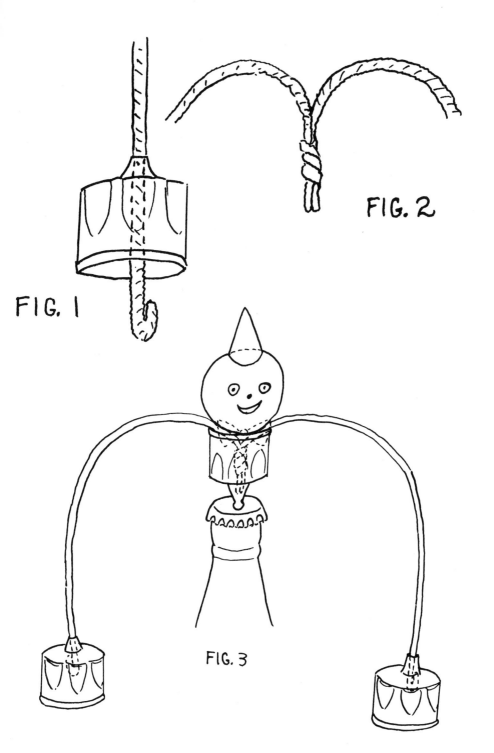

FIG. 1

FIG. 2

FIG. 3

MARBLE TRIVET

A bag of marbles may be quickly turned into a trivet for hold-ing a hot dish or a teapot. It makes a nice mat to use under a potted plant, too.

You Will Need:

Marbles, either solid color, "cat's eye" or variegated

The lid from a 5-pound syrup can

Clear household cement

How to Make It:

Arrange the marbles in the recessed top of the can lid to decide on a design you like. Two are shown in Figs. 1 and 2. You may copy these or design your own. After you have an arrangement you like, make a sketch on paper so you will re-member how to place the different marbles. Remove the marbles from the lid.

Glue the marbles to the lid, putting them around the out-side rim first, then working towards the center until the lid is filled in.

If you wish, you can paint the lid before gluing in the marbles. Gold, copper or any color of enamel makes an attrac-tive background.

Let the trivet dry overnight to be sure the glue is set, before using it.

FIG. 1

FIG. 2

CAN CANISTERS

Cans with snap-on plastic lids, such as coffee cans in several sizes and three pound shortening cans can be quickly turned into a set of attractive canisters for mom's cabinet top.

You Will Need:

Empty tin cans with snap-on lids

"Contact" plastic, one design to cover the cans and a small piece of a solid color for the letters.

Ruler

Scissors

How to Make It:

Cut Contact to cover each can. The piece should be as wide as the can is tall between the rims, and long enough to wrap around the can and lap over itself about 1 inch.

If there are paper labels on the outsides of the cans, remove them. Wash and dry the cans.

Remove the paper backing from the Contact and wrap it around the can. Be sure there are no wrinkles in the Contact.

Cut strips of the solid color Contact 1/4 inch wide, for the letters. Cut the strips into pieces as needed. Make the letters 1 inch tall.

Stick the strips to the can, lapping the edges to form the letters. Fig. 1 shows how to put on the strips to make the letter S. Others are formed in the same manner.

Arrange the letters in a slanting line from the top to the bottom of the canister to spell the word. Fig. 2 shows how the letters are arranged on the "Tea" can.

116

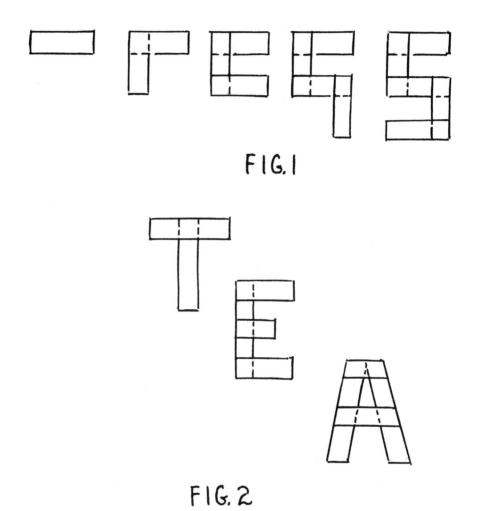

FIG. 1

FIG. 2

WIND TINKLER

The Japanese make wind bells of bamboo and hang them in the garden to frighten the birds away from their crops. This one is just to make a pleasant tinkling sound when the breezes blow.

You Will Need:

Heavy crochet thread—9 pieces each 18 inches long.

A plastic lid from a cottage cheese carton

36 pop bottle caps

A hammer, small nail and a small block of wood.

How to Make It:

Punch a small hole through the center of the plastic lid. Punch 8 holes around the rim, 1/4 inch from the edge and equal distances apart, Fig. 1.

Remove the cork liners from the bottle caps.

Punch a hole through the center of the cap by laying the cap, top down, on the block of wood and using the nail and hammer to make the hole.

Pass the end of a piece of thread through the hole in a bottle cap and knot the string around the edge of the cap, as in Fig. 2.

2 inches above the cap, tie a knot in the string, Fig. 2.

Pass the free end of the string through the hole in a second bottle cap, from the inside to the outside—Fig. 2. Push the cap down against the knot, then tie another knot in the string just above the cap to keep it in position.

2 inches higher up on the string tie another knot, put on another cap and tie a knot. Tie another knot 2 inches higher, put on a cap and tie a knot.

Prepare 8 more strings each with four caps, in the same way. Tie a knot in each string 4 inches above the last cap.

Pass the end of a string through each hole in the plastic carton lid. Push the lid down on the strings until it rests on the knots. Tie a knot in each string just above the lid to hold it in position.

Gather all the strings together and tie all 9 into a knot to hold them together—Fig. 3.

Clip off the extra length of threads a bit above the knot and tie on a single thread for hanging.

Hang up the tinkler under the porch roof or anywhere that it will swing free when the wind blows. The caps will strike against each other to make pleasant tinkly music.

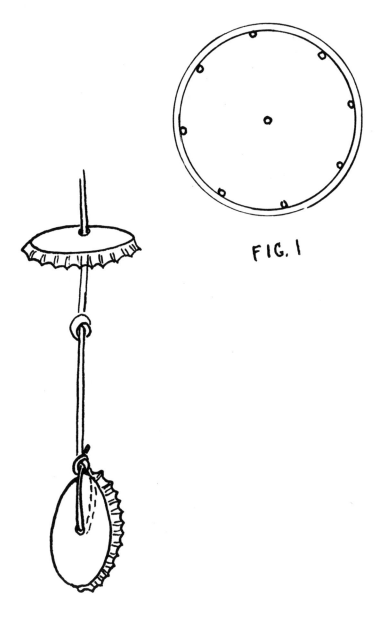

FIG. 1

FIG. 2

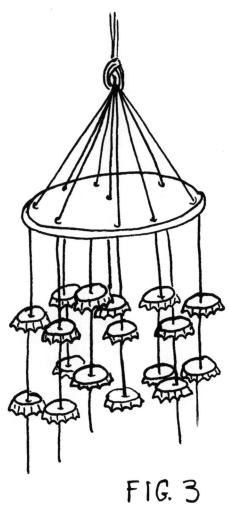

FIG. 3

MATCHBOX TREASURE CHEST

Need something to keep your necklaces in? Or your collection of arrowheads or Indian head pennies? This chest with sliding drawers is just the thing. It is handy for keeping any number of different things.

You Will Need:

Empty match boxes   Wooden beads

Gift wrap paper   White glue

How to Make It:

Glue the covers of three match boxes together, one on top of another, Fig. 3.

Decorate one end of each box. You may paint on a design like those shown in Fig. 1 or 2. Or you may cut a small picture from a magazine ad and glue that in place. The decoration depends on what you want to store in your chest.

Cut a piece of gift wrap paper as wide as the box covers are long, and long enough to wrap around the stack of three and lap 1/2 inch.

Glue the gift wrap paper around the stack of boxes, lapping the ends at the bottom, as shown in Fig. 4.

Glue a wooden bead to the front of each box for a knob.

If you want to make a larger chest, glue more boxes together. A six-drawer chest can be made by gluing two stacks of three together, side by side, before covering with the gift wrap. You can make a four-drawer chest by gluing two boxes together instead of three and gluing two stacks side by side. A lower six-drawer chest may be made with three two-box stacks.

FIG. 1   FIG. 2

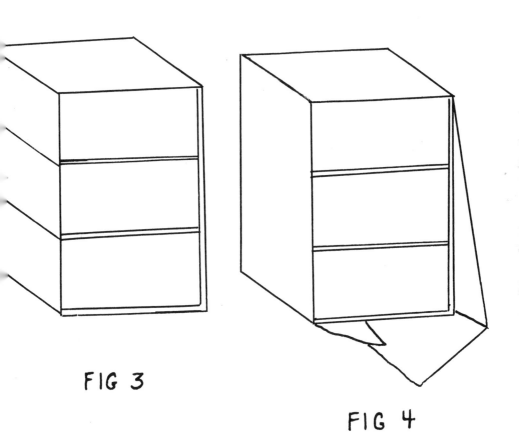

FIG 3

FIG 4

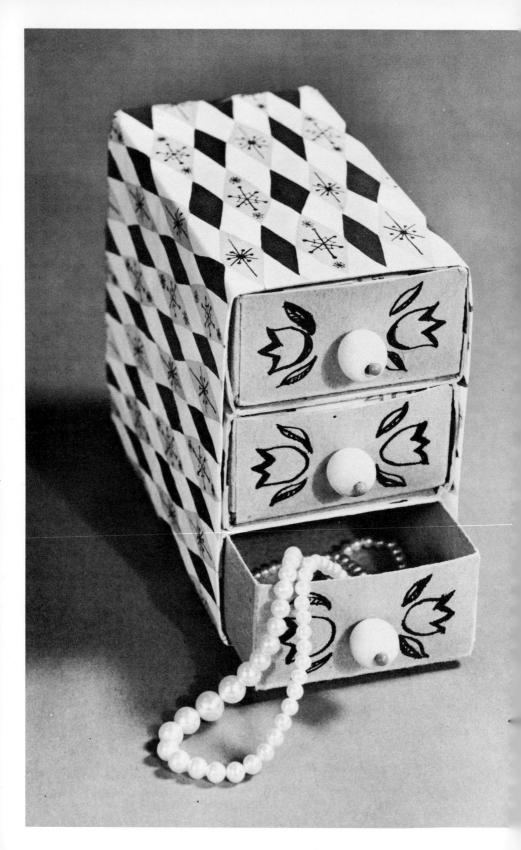

PLANT BIRDS

These little birds won't sing but they look pretty sitting on perches among the potted plants.

You Will Need:

Peanuts   Taffy apple sticks—or swab sticks

Drawing paper   Flat toothpicks   Glue

How to Make It:

Use peanuts for the bodies of the birds. Choose those with two or three nuts in the shell. Those with only one nut are too short.

Lay out the topknot, tail and two wings on drawing paper, like the patterns given. Fig. 1. Remember that the two wings must lie in opposite directions to fit the two sides of the bird.

Paint the "feathers" on the paper. Also paint the peanut body for your bird. You may use either water colors or hobby enamels.

Cut the topknot and tail along the heavy lines to separate the "feathers."

Roll each "feather" around a toothpick to make it curl, Fig. 2.

Glue the topknot, wings and tail to the peanut body.

Use a short piece of flat toothpick for the beak. Make a hole through the peanut shell with a darning needle and push the beak in place.

Punch a hole through the shell in the center bottom of the body.

Sharpen both ends of the stick in the pencil sharpener. Dip one end in glue and push it into the hole in the body.

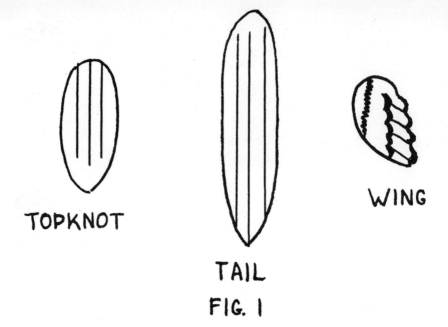

TOPKNOT

TAIL
FIG. 1

WING

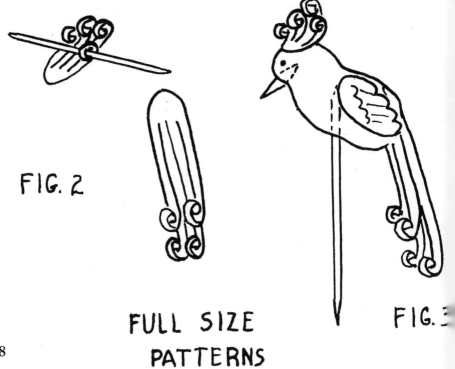

FIG. 2

FULL SIZE
PATTERNS

FIG. 3

QUICKIE WREN HOUSE

Wrens, those cheerful little songsters that like to live near people, aren't at all fussy about their houses. They'll nest in tin cans or gourds or coconut shells. Here's a house that's so quick and easy you'll want to make several to hang in trees around the yard.

You Will Need:

A half gallon paper milk carton

Light cardboard (shoe box, cereal box—)

Adhesive backed plastic (Contact) in wood grain finish

Stapler

Wire or cord for hanging

How to Make It:

Rinse the milk carton. Turn it upside down to drain and dry.

When the inside is dry, fold the spout shut and staple the edges together.

Cover the carton with Contact. Some wood grain Contact even has a rough finish so it feels as well as looks like wood. Wrens like that especially well.

Cut a piece of cardboard the size shown in Fig. 1. Lay a straight edge ruler along the center line and make a crease along the line with the tip of a knife blade. Also crease along the lines on each side of the center.

Bend the cardboard on the center line. Bend in the other direction along each of the other two lines to get the shape shown in Fig. 2. This is the roof.

Cut a piece of Contact 6 inches wide, 8 1/2 inches long and cover the roof piece allowing the Contact to extend 1/2 inch beyond the cardboard all around. Fold the Contact around the edge and stick it to the under side of the roof.

Glue the roof to the slant top of the milk carton. Punch two holes through roof and top edge of the carton. Thread the wire or cord through for hanging, Fig. 3.

About halfway down on the front of the house, cut out a 1 inch diameter circle for a door.

Hang the house 8 to 10 feet above the ground.

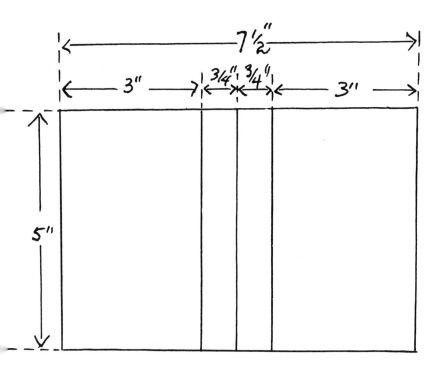

FIG. 1

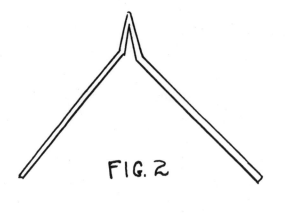

FIG. 2

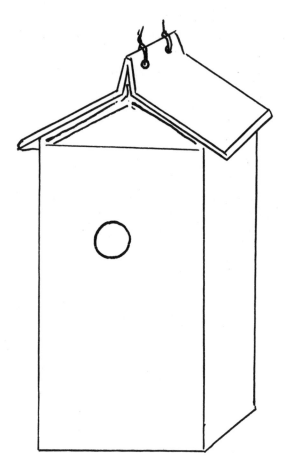

FIG. 3

NATURE NOTES

You can decorate plain note paper or correspondence cards with "leaves under glass." If you wish, you can make your own cards from plain paper.

You Will Need:

Note paper, correspondence cards or plain paper and envelopes

Small leaves

Typing paper

Transparent "Contact"

White glue

India ink

How to Make It:

The leaves should be small enough to fit on paper measuring 1 1/4 inch wide and 1 3/4 inches long. Press the leaves between the pages of a magazine for several hours to make them lie flat.

Cut pieces of typing paper 1 1/4 inch wide, 1 3/4 inches long, and pieces of transparent Contact the same size. Leave the paper backing on the Contact for the time being.

Lay a leaf on a piece of typing paper. Peel the backing off the Contact and lay the Contact over the leaf onto the paper, Fig. 1. Press the Contact and the paper together all around the leaf.

Make as many more "leaves under glass" as you want to use.

Glue the leaf in the upper left corner of the note paper or correspondence card.

With pen and india ink, draw a black border around the leaf paper. Do not use a ruler but draw freehand "wavy" lines.

If you're making your own notes from plain paper, cut the paper to the size shown in Fig. 2 or Fig. 4. Fold it in half to get the notes shown in Fig. 3 and Fig. 5.

Figure 6. and Fig. 7 show completed notes.

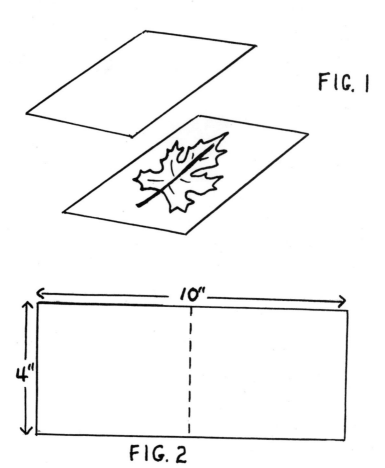

FIG. 1

10"

4"

FIG. 2

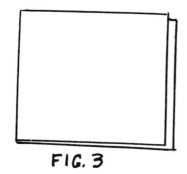

FIG. 3

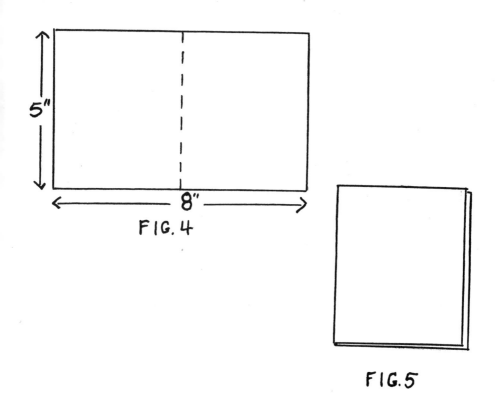

5"

8"

FIG. 4

FIG.5

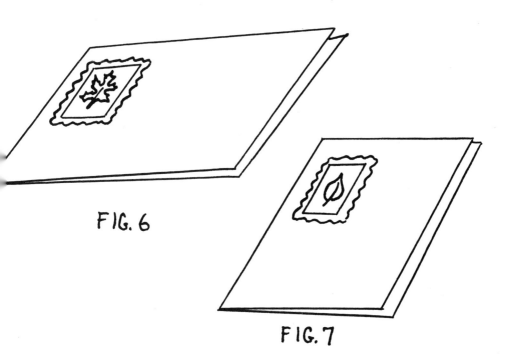

FIG. 6

FIG. 7